WHERE AM I?

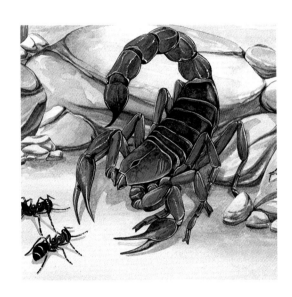

This is a rocky place.
It is hot and dry.

WHERE AM I?

By Moira Butterfield

Illustrated by
Stephanie and Simon Calder

Thameside Press

Distributed in the United States by
Smart Apple Media
123 South Broad Street
Mankato, Minnesota 56001

Editor: Honor Head
Designer: Helen James
Illustrators: Stephanie and Simon Calder
Map illustration: Robin Carter / Wildlife Art Agency
Consultant: Steve Pollock

Printed in China

ISBN: 1-929298-35-8
Library of Congress Catalog Card Number: 99-73407

Where am I
in the world?
Read this book
and see if you
can guess.

A scorpion lives
here. See if you
can find it in
the pictures.

This place is very hot
in the daytime.

There are lots of rocks and
stones on the ground. Under
the rocks are cool, shadowy
places where ants and other
insects like to crawl around.

Can you see a scorpion curling its tail over its back? There is a sharp stinger on the end of its tail.

It is very dry here.
It hardly ever rains.

The plants that grow
here are spiky and
tough. They are good
at living without very
much water.

Some animals get the water they need by eating the plants. Point to a tortoise munching on a plant.

Animals need to stay cool in the heat.

Spadefoot toads have big feet. They dig burrows in the ground and hide inside, away from the hot sun.

The tortoise has a long tongue so it can lick its head and shoulders. The spit helps to keep it cool.

Fat, juicy plants called cacti grow here.

A cactus can store lots
of water inside its stem.
Its roots suck up the
water from the ground.

Can you see a cactus with long, prickly thorns all over it? The thorns will stick in any animal that tries to take a bite.

It gets much colder at night when the sun goes down.

Then lots of animals come out of their underground burrows. It's a good time for them to find food.

Can you see three kangaroo rats, a burrowing owl, and a white-tailed antelope squirrel looking for food?

There are lots of hunters looking for animals to eat.

A furry kit fox is prowling around looking for a rat or a mouse that will make a tasty meal.

Can you point to a roadrunner chasing a lizard? It does not fly well and prefers to run after its food.

Some of the animals that live here are poisonous.

The gila monster has bright
colors to warn others that
it has a poisonous bite.
It likes to eat birds' eggs.

A tarantula spider can grab a bird or an insect in its pincers and give it a deadly poisonous bite.

Some animals have clever ways to scare their enemies.

A frightened skunk stands on its front legs to shoot a horrible stinking spray over its enemy.

A rattlesnake rattles the end of its tail to warn enemies away. If the enemy comes too close, the snake will give it a deadly bite.

Lots of birds live here.

Some of the birds are hunters. Can you see a red-tailed hawk with long, sharp talons for catching mice?

A gila woodpecker
has made a hole
in a cactus. This
is a good place
to build a nest.

There are big animals here too.

Mule deer munch the spiky grasses and plants. Can you see a mother deer with her baby? It is called a fawn.

Coyotes live in gangs called packs. When evening comes they howl to each other in the moonlight.

Do you know where I am?

I am in a North American desert.

Some deserts are made up of hundreds of miles of sand. A North American desert doesn't have much sand, but it is very dry and covered in rocks and stones.

Here is a map
of the world.

There are deserts
all around the
world.

The deserts are
colored pink.

North America

I am here.

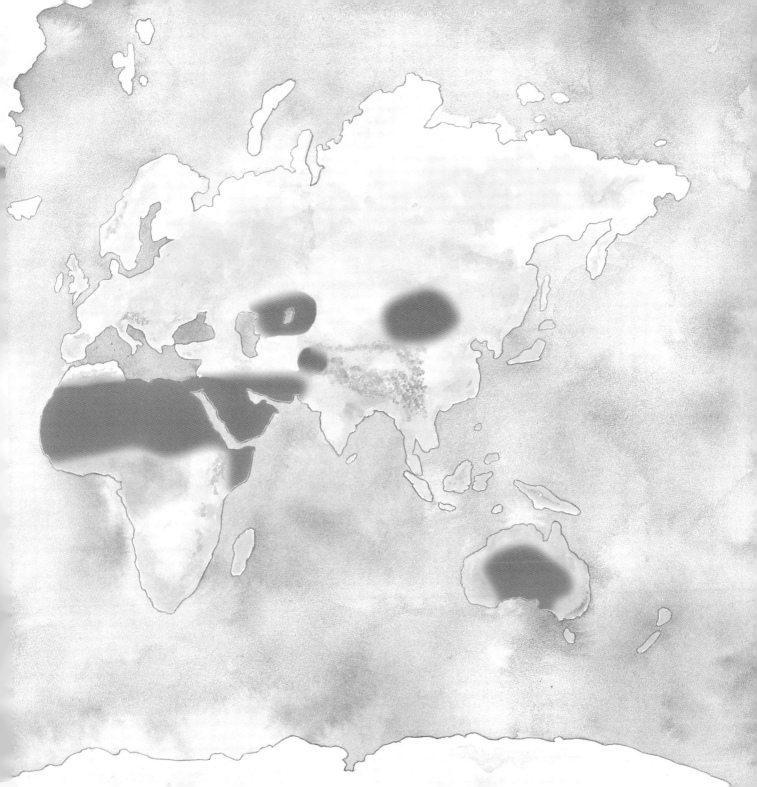

Where are these plants and animals?
Turn the pages back to find them.

Desert lilies

Jackrabbits

Chuckwalla lizard

Brazilian free-tailed bats

Barrel cacti

Prairie falcon

Ravens

Cactus wren

Prickly pear cactus

Ruby-throated hummingbird

Animal facts

The turkey vulture can see much farther than a human can. It circles in the desert sky, looking for dead creatures to eat.

The kit fox eats small animals such as rabbits and lizards. Its huge ears help it hear every small sound in the desert.

The kangaroo rat hops across the desert. It never drinks water. It gets all its water from eating desert plants and cacti.

Scorpions catch insects in their claws. They sting the insect if it is very big. They crush their food and suck it up.

The burrowing owl makes its nest in a hole in the ground. It stays in its nest during the day and hunts at night.

The desert tortoise stays out in the scorching sun. When it gets too hot, it wets its back legs to cool down.